Understanding Todays Digital Marketing

Master Every Strategy, Tool, and Trend for Digital Marketing In Modern Times

Bob Ondijo

COPYRIGHT

© 2024 Bob Ondijo. All rights reserved.

No part of this book may be reproduced, distributed, or transmitted in any form or by any means, including photocopying, recording, or other electronic or mechanical methods, without the prior written permission of the publisher, except in the case of brief quotations embodied in critical reviews and certain other noncommercial uses permitted by copyright law. For permission requests, write to the publisher, addressed "Attention: Permissions Coordinator," at the address below.

Publisher's Name: Bob Ondijo

Publisher's Address: P.O.Box 29771-00100 Nairobi, Kenya

Ordering Information: Special discounts are available on quantity purchases by corporations, associations, and others. For details, contact the publisher at the address above.

Printed in the United States of America

First Edition, 2024

Acknowledgements

Acknowledgments

This work is the culmination of a lifetime of personal learning and development, enriched by the collective contributions of numerous mentors, teachers, supporters, advisors, friends, and family. I am constantly aware that we are the sum total of what we have learned, as well as the beneficiaries of the contributions made by so many others as we journey towards our ultimate destiny.

No achievement in life is accomplished without the help of many known and unknown individuals who have influenced our lives. We owe every measure of our success to the array of input from so many. Here are just a few who made this work possible:

First and foremost, let this begin with gratitude to God the ultimate giver of life.

Secondly, am deeply grateful to my beloved wife, Esther Kamene Kathini, for her unwavering support, love, and encouragement throughout this journey. Your patience and understanding have been my greatest strength.

To my sons, Phinehas Prince and Peniel Bob, you are my inspiration. Your curiosity and zest for life continually motivate me to strive for excellence.

A special thanks to Dr. Ope Banwo, whose introduction to mass digital entrepreneurship, mass self employment initiative through fish for life program Nigeria inspired me. Your mentorship and guidance have paved the way for many opportunities and growth in this digital era.

Thank you all for your invaluable contributions to this journey.

Bob Ondijo

About the author

Bob Ondijo is a multifaceted real estate wealth advisor and serial entrepreneur who also excels as a digital entrepreneur, digital marketer, and visionary Bookpreneur. As a Coach and Digital Expert, he is a motivational speaker and teacher renowned for his innovative use of AI in the publishing sector. Bob's academic journey is marked by excellence, holding a degree in geology from the University of Nairobi, Kenya.

As the founder of Estbonites Publishing, Bob has revolutionized the way books are authored, published, and marketed, emphasizing the power of digital tools to reach global audiences. His efforts have significantly impacted the digital business landscape, demonstrating how to make money online through effective strategies.

With a prolific career spanning several industries, Bob Ondijo has authored numerous published works, establishing himself as a best-selling author in personal development, leadership, and business & entrepreneurship domains. His literary contributions include notable titles such as *Skillpreneur, Passionpreneur, Potentialpreneur, Knowledgepreneur, Talentpreneur, Experiencepreneur, Expertizepreneur, Successpreneur, Failurepreneur, and Blogpreneur.*

Through his publishing house, Bob Ondijo has nurtured a generation of authors, empowering them with the knowledge to navigate the digital landscape successfully. His role as a 'Digital Maven' is underscored by his dedication to digital transformation and education, guiding individuals and businesses alike toward harnessing the opportunities of the digital age. Bob's expertise in digital marketing, digital products creation, digital business, AI, and global digital trends has made him a sought-after coach and speaker. He offers strategies for digital entrepreneurship success in the rapidly evolving digital economy.

With a career dedicated to raising digital literacy and fostering self-employment, Bob Ondijo continues to be a pivotal figure in shaping the future of digital business, AI, digital publishing, and content creation.

Contents

Acknowledgements 3
Introduction 1
Chapter 1: Understanding Digital Marketing 1
Chapter 2: How To Build a Strong Online Presence 6
Chapter 3: The best way to do Search Engine Optimization (SEO) in modern times 13
Chapter 4: The best way to do Content Marketing in modern times 19
Chapter 5: The best way to do Social Media Marketing in modern times 24
Chapter 6: The best way to do Email Marketing in modern times 31
Chapter 7: Pay-Per-Click (PPC) Advertising 38
Chapter 8: Analytics and Data-Driven Marketing 45
Chapter 9: Trends and Innovations in Digital Marketing 51
Chapter 10: Creating an Integrated Digital Marketing Strategy 57
Chapter 11: The best way to do Facebook Marketing in modern times 63
Chapter 12: The best way to do TikTok Marketing in modern times 72
Chapter 13: The best way to do Instagram Marketing in modern times 76
Chapter 14: The best way to do YouTube Marketing in modern times 80
Chapter 15: How to do Video Marketing in modern times 86
Chapter 16: The best way to do LinkedIn Marketing in modern times 92

Chapter 17: Marketing Consultant 96
Chapter 18: Managing Your Online Reputation 102
Conclusion 108
Appendix 113

Introduction

The Importance of Digital Marketing

Digital marketing has become an indispensable component of any successful business strategy. In today's interconnected world, where the majority of consumers are online, businesses must meet their customers where they are. Digital marketing not only provides a platform for businesses to promote their products and services, but it also offers invaluable insights into consumer behavior, preferences, and trends. This comprehensive approach to marketing allows businesses to reach a broader audience, engage with customers in real-time, and measure the effectiveness of their marketing campaigns with precision.

4 reasons why Digital marketing is crucial:

1. **Global Reach:** Unlike traditional marketing methods, digital marketing enables businesses to reach a global audience. With the click of a button, companies can connect with potential customers from different parts of the world.

2. **Cost-Effectiveness:** Digital marketing is often more cost-effective than traditional marketing. It allows businesses to allocate their marketing budget more efficiently, targeting specific demographics and minimizing wasted expenditure.

3. **Measurable Results:** One of the most significant advantages of digital marketing is the ability to track and measure results in real-time. Businesses can monitor key performance indicators (KPIs) such as

website traffic, conversion rates, and return on investment (ROI), allowing for data-driven decision-making.

4. **Customer Engagement:** Digital marketing facilitates direct interaction with customers through social media, email marketing, and other online channels. This engagement helps build strong customer relationships and fosters brand loyalty.

Overview of Digital Marketing Strategies and Tools

To harness the full potential of digital marketing, businesses must employ a variety of strategies and tools. Here is an overview of the most essential ones:

1. **Search Engine Optimization (SEO):**
   - **Definition:** SEO involves optimizing a website to rank higher in search engine results pages (SERPs).
   - **Components:** On-page SEO (keywords, meta tags, content quality), off-page SEO (backlinks, social signals), and technical SEO (site speed, mobile-friendliness).

2. **Content Marketing:**
   - **Definition:** Content marketing focuses on creating and distributing valuable, relevant content to attract and engage a target audience.
   - **Formats:** Blog posts, videos, infographics, podcasts, eBooks.

3. **Social Media Marketing:**
    - **Definition:** Social media marketing leverages platforms like Facebook, Instagram, Twitter, and LinkedIn to promote products and services.
    - **Tactics:** Organic posts, paid ads, influencer collaborations, community engagement.

4. **Email Marketing:**
    - **Definition:** Email marketing involves sending targeted emails to a subscriber list to promote products, share updates, or nurture leads.
    - **Best Practices:** Personalization, segmentation, A/B testing, automation.

5. **Pay-Per-Click (PPC) Advertising:**
    - **Definition:** PPC advertising allows businesses to display ads on search engines and other platforms, paying a fee each time the ad is clicked.
    - **Platforms:** Google Ads, Bing Ads, social media ads.

6. **Affiliate Marketing:**
    - **Definition:** Affiliate marketing involves partnering with affiliates who promote a business's products in exchange for a commission on sales.
    - **Networks:** Amazon Associates, ShareASale, CJ Affiliate.

7. **Influencer Marketing:**
    - **Definition:** Influencer marketing leverages individuals with a significant online following to promote products.
    - **Approach:** Identifying relevant influencers, negotiating collaborations, tracking performance.

8. **Analytics and Reporting:**
    - **Importance:** Analytics tools help businesses track the performance of their digital marketing efforts and make data-driven decisions.
    - **Tools:** Google Analytics, SEMrush, Moz, HubSpot.

How to Use This Book

This book is designed to be a comprehensive guide to mastering digital marketing strategies and tools. Whether you are a beginner or an experienced marketer, you will find valuable insights and practical advice to enhance your digital marketing efforts. Here's how to make the most of this book:

1. **Start with the Basics:** If you are new to digital marketing, begin with the foundational chapters that cover essential concepts and terminology.
2. **Dive into Specific Strategies:** Each chapter delves into a different digital marketing strategy, providing

detailed explanations, step-by-step guides, and best practices.

3. **Implement Actionable Tips:** Throughout the book, you will find actionable tips and techniques that you can implement immediately to improve your digital marketing campaigns.

4. **Use Case Studies and Examples:** Learn from real-world case studies and examples that illustrate successful digital marketing tactics and campaigns.

5. **Leverage Tools and Resources:** Take advantage of the recommended tools and resources to streamline your digital marketing efforts and achieve better results.

6. **Track Your Progress:** Use the metrics and analytics discussed in the book to monitor your progress and make data-driven adjustments to your strategies.

By following the guidance in this book, you will be well-equipped to navigate the ever-evolving digital marketing landscape and drive success for your business.

Chapter 1: Understanding Digital Marketing

Definition and Scope of Digital Marketing

Digital marketing refers to the utilization of digital channels, platforms, and technologies to promote products, services, or brands to a target audience. Unlike traditional marketing methods, digital marketing leverages the internet and electronic devices, making it possible to reach consumers in a more interactive and personalized manner. The scope of digital marketing is broad, encompassing various strategies and tactics aimed at engaging customers, driving traffic, and generating leads or sales.

8 Key aspects of digital marketing:

- **Search Engine Optimization (SEO):** Enhancing website visibility on search engines like Google.

- **Content Marketing:** Creating valuable content to attract and retain a clearly defined audience.

- **Social Media Marketing:** Leveraging platforms like Facebook, Twitter, and Instagram to reach and engage customers.

- **Email Marketing:** Sending targeted emails to prospects and customers.

- **Pay-Per-Click (PPC) Advertising:** Paying for ads that appear on search engines and other platforms.
- **Affiliate Marketing:** Partnering with affiliates to promote products for a commission.
- **Influencer Marketing:** Collaborating with influential individuals to reach their followers.
- **Analytics and Reporting:** Tracking and analyzing data to measure the effectiveness of marketing efforts.

The Evolution of Digital Marketing

Digital marketing has undergone significant transformations since its inception. The journey began with the advent of the internet, which opened new avenues for marketers to reach audiences in unprecedented ways. Here's a brief timeline of its evolution:

1. **The 1990s:** The birth of the internet marked the beginning of digital marketing. Websites became the primary digital marketing tools, with banner ads being the first form of online advertising.

2. **The 2000s:** The rise of search engines like Google introduced SEO, and the emergence of social media platforms like Facebook and LinkedIn revolutionized how businesses connected with consumers. Email marketing also gained popularity during this period.

3. **The 2010s:** Mobile devices became ubiquitous, leading to the rise of mobile marketing. Content marketing, social media marketing, and influencer

marketing also became essential components of digital marketing strategies.

4. **The 2020s:** Advances in technology, such as artificial intelligence (AI) and big data, have further transformed digital marketing. AI-driven tools now enable more personalized and efficient marketing campaigns, while data analytics allows for deeper insights into consumer behavior.

7 Key Components of Digital Marketing

To effectively implement digital marketing strategies, businesses must focus on several key components:

1. **Search Engine Optimization (SEO):**
    - **On-Page SEO:** Optimizing individual web pages to rank higher in search engine results.
    - **Off-Page SEO:** Building backlinks and increasing site authority through external efforts.
    - **Technical SEO:** Enhancing the technical aspects of a website, such as site speed and mobile-friendliness.

2. **Content Marketing:**
    - **Content Creation:** Developing high quality content, including blogs, videos, infographics, and eBooks.
    - **Content Distribution:** Sharing content across various platforms to reach a broader audience.

- o **Content Strategy:** Planning and managing content to achieve specific business goals.

3. **Social Media Marketing:**

    - o **Platform Selection:** Choosing the right social media platforms based on the target audience.
    - o **Content Planning:** Creating engaging content tailored for each platform.
    - o **Community Management:** Interacting with followers and managing the brand's online presence.

4. **Email Marketing:**

    - o **List Building:** Collecting email addresses through opt-ins and lead magnets.
    - o **Campaign Creation:** Designing and sending targeted email campaigns.
    - o **Analytics:** Tracking open rates, click-through rates, and conversions to measure campaign success.

5. **Pay-Per-Click (PPC) Advertising:**

    - o **Ad Creation:** Developing compelling ads that attract clicks.
    - o **Keyword Research:** Identifying the right keywords to target.
    - o **Campaign Management:** Monitoring and optimizing ad performance to maximize ROI.

6. **Analytics and Reporting:**
    - **Data Collection:** Using tools like Google Analytics to gather data on website traffic and user behavior.
    - **Performance Tracking:** Measuring key metrics such as bounce rates, conversion rates, and customer acquisition costs.
    - **Data-Driven Decisions:** Making informed decisions based on data analysis to improve marketing strategies.
7. **Affiliate and Influencer Marketing:**
    - **Partner Selection:** Choosing affiliates and influencers who align with the brand.
    - **Campaign Collaboration:** Working with partners to create authentic and effective marketing campaigns.
    - **Performance Monitoring:** Tracking the results of affiliate and influencer campaigns to ensure they meet business objectives.

By understanding these fundamental components, businesses can create comprehensive digital marketing strategies that effectively engage their target audience, drive traffic, and achieve their marketing goals.

Chapter 2: How To Build a Strong Online Presence

Creating a User-Friendly Website

In the digital age, your website is often the first point of contact between your brand and potential customers. Therefore, it is crucial to create a user-friendly website that provides a seamless and engaging experience for visitors.

6 key elements to consider:

1. **Intuitive Navigation:**
    - Ensure that your website has a clear and straightforward navigation structure. Use descriptive menu labels and organize content logically, so users can easily find what they are looking for.
    - Implement a search bar to help users quickly locate specific information.

2. **Responsive Design:**
    - Design your website to be responsive, meaning it should adapt to different screen sizes and devices, such as desktops, tablets, and smartphones.

- Use flexible grids, layouts, and media queries to ensure that your website looks and functions well on all devices.

3. **Fast Loading Times:**
    - Optimize your website's performance to reduce loading times. Compress images, leverage browser caching, and minimize the use of heavy scripts.
    - A fast-loading website improves user experience and positively impacts your search engine rankings.

4. **Clear Calls to Action (CTAs):**
    - Use prominent and compelling CTAs to guide users towards desired actions, such as signing up for a newsletter, making a purchase, or contacting you.
    - Ensure that CTAs stand out visually and are strategically placed throughout your website.

5. **Accessible Design:**
    - Design your website to be accessible to all users, including those with disabilities. Follow web accessibility guidelines, such as providing alt text for images, using proper heading structures, and ensuring keyboard navigability.
    - Accessibility not only broadens your audience but also enhances your site's usability for everyone.

6. **High-Quality Content:**
    - Provide valuable, relevant, and engaging content that addresses your audience's needs and interests.
    - Use a mix of text, images, videos, and infographics to keep users engaged and encourage them to spend more time on your site.
    -

5 Importance of Mobile Optimization

With the increasing use of smartphones and tablets, mobile optimization has become a critical aspect of building a strong online presence. Here's why it's essential:

1. **Growing Mobile Usage:**
    - A significant portion of web traffic now comes from mobile devices. Ensuring your website is mobile-friendly helps you reach a broader audience.
    - Mobile users expect a seamless browsing experience, and a non-optimized site can lead to high bounce rates.
2. **Improved User Experience:**
    - Mobile optimization enhances the overall user experience by providing a site that is

easy to navigate and interact with on smaller screens.
- Features such as touch-friendly buttons, readable text without zooming, and quick load times contribute to a positive mobile experience.

3. **Higher Search Rankings:**
    - Search engines like Google prioritize mobile-friendly websites in their search results. A mobile-optimized site can improve your search engine rankings and increase visibility.
    - Implementing mobile-first indexing ensures that your site is crawled and indexed based on its mobile version.

4. **Competitive Advantage:**
    - Businesses with mobile-optimized websites are more likely to attract and retain customers compared to those with poorly optimized sites.
    - A mobile-friendly site demonstrates that your brand is modern, user-focused, and responsive to technological trends.

5. **Increased Conversions:**
    - Mobile optimization can lead to higher conversion rates as users find it easier to navigate, explore products, and complete transactions on their devices.

- Streamlined checkout processes and mobile payment options enhance the purchasing experience.

Crafting a Compelling Brand Identity

A compelling brand identity is essential for differentiating your business from competitors and creating a lasting impression on your audience.

6 key components to consider:

1. **Brand Values and Mission:**
   - Clearly define your brand's values, mission, and vision. Communicate what your brand stands for and what it aims to achieve.
   - Ensure that these elements resonate with your target audience and reflect their values and aspirations.

2. **Consistent Visual Identity:**
   - Develop a cohesive visual identity that includes a logo, color palette, typography, and design elements. Consistency in visuals helps in brand recognition and builds trust.
   - Use these elements consistently across all marketing materials, including your website, social media profiles, and printed materials.

3. **Authentic Brand Voice:**
   - Establish a distinctive brand voice that reflects your brand's personality and values. Whether it's formal, friendly, witty, or

- authoritative, ensure it is authentic and consistent across all communication channels.
  - Engage with your audience in a way that feels genuine and relatable.

4. **Compelling Storytelling:**
    - Craft and share your brand's story in a way that connects emotionally with your audience. Highlight the journey, challenges, and successes that define your brand.
    - Use storytelling to humanize your brand and build deeper connections with your customers.

5. **Customer-Centric Approach:**
    - Focus on understanding and addressing your customers' needs, preferences, and pain points. Show empathy and prioritize customer satisfaction in all your interactions.
    - Collect and leverage customer feedback to continuously improve your products, services, and overall customer experience.

6. **Engagement and Interaction:**
    - Actively engage with your audience through social media, email marketing, and other channels. Respond to comments, messages, and reviews promptly and thoughtfully.
    - Foster a sense of community around your brand by encouraging user-generated

content, hosting events, and participating in relevant conversations.

By following these principles, you can build a strong online presence that attracts and retains customers, enhances brand loyalty, and drives business growth.

Chapter 3: The best way to do Search Engine Optimization (SEO) in modern times

Introduction to SEO

Search Engine Optimization, commonly known as SEO, is the practice of optimizing a website to improve its visibility and ranking on search engine results pages (SERPs). The primary objective of SEO is to increase organic (non-paid) traffic to a website by enhancing its relevance and authority in the eyes of search engines like Google, Bing, and Yahoo. SEO involves various strategies and techniques that align with the algorithms used by search engines to rank web pages.

The significance of SEO cannot be overstated. In an era where digital presence determines business success, SEO serves as a critical tool for driving traffic, increasing brand awareness, and ultimately, boosting revenue. By understanding and implementing SEO best practices, businesses can ensure their target audience finds them when searching for relevant products or services online.

On-Page and Off-Page SEO Techniques

SEO is broadly categorized into two main areas: On-Page SEO and Off-Page SEO. Each plays a pivotal role in enhancing a website's search engine ranking.

On-Page SEO:

On-Page SEO refers to the optimization of individual web pages to rank higher and earn more relevant traffic. Key components of On-Page SEO include:

- **Title Tags:** Crafting compelling and keyword-rich titles that accurately reflect the content of the page.

- **Meta Descriptions:** Writing concise and descriptive meta descriptions that encourage users to click through to the site.

- **Header Tags (H1, H2, H3, etc.):** Using header tags to structure content, making it easier for search engines to understand the hierarchy and importance of information.

- **Content Quality:** Creating high-quality, informative, and engaging content that provides value to users.

- **Keyword Placement:** Strategically incorporating keywords into the content, including titles, headers, and body text, without keyword stuffing.

- **URL Structure:** Designing clean and descriptive URLs that include relevant keywords.

- **Internal Linking:** Linking to other pages within the same website to improve navigation and distribute link equity.

- **Image Optimization:** Using descriptive file names and alt text for images to improve search engine understanding and indexing of visual content.

- **Mobile Friendliness:** Ensuring the website is responsive and provides a good user experience on mobile devices.

- **Page Load Speed:** Optimizing the website to load quickly, as page speed is a critical ranking factor.

Off-Page SEO:

Off-Page SEO involves activities conducted outside the website to improve its search engine ranking. Key components of Off-Page SEO include:

- **Backlink Building:** Acquiring high-quality backlinks from reputable websites to increase the site's authority and credibility.

- **Social Media Engagement:** Promoting content on social media platforms to drive traffic and encourage sharing.

- **Guest Blogging:** Writing and publishing articles on other reputable websites to gain exposure and backlinks.

- **Influencer Outreach:** Collaborating with influencers to amplify content reach and acquire backlinks.

- **Online Directories and Listings:** Submitting the website to relevant online directories and business listings to improve visibility.

- **Content Marketing:** Creating and distributing valuable content across various platforms to attract and engage a target audience.

Keyword Research and Implementation

Keyword research is a fundamental aspect of SEO. It involves identifying the terms and phrases that potential customers use when searching for products or services related to the business. Effective keyword research allows businesses to understand their audience's search behavior and tailor their content to meet those needs.

Steps for Conducting Keyword Research:

1. **Brainstorm Seed Keywords:** Start with broad terms related to the business, products, or services.
2. **Use Keyword Research Tools:** Utilize tools like Google Keyword Planner, SEMrush, Ahrefs, and Moz to find related keywords and gather data on search volume, competition, and trends.
3. **Analyze Competitors:** Look at competitors' websites to identify the keywords they are targeting and ranking for.
4. **Focus on Long-Tail Keywords:** Long-tail keywords are longer, more specific phrases that often have lower competition and higher conversion rates.
5. **Group and Prioritize Keywords:** Organize keywords into groups based on relevance and prioritize them based on search volume and business goals.

Implementing Keywords:

- **Content Creation:** Develop content that naturally incorporates target keywords, providing valuable information that addresses user intent.
- **On-Page Elements:** Include keywords in title tags, meta descriptions, header tags, and throughout the content.
- **URL Structure:** Use keywords in URLs to make them descriptive and SEO-friendly.
- **Internal Linking:** Use keyword-rich anchor text for internal links to improve site navigation and keyword relevance.

Tools for SEO Success

Various tools and resources are available to assist with SEO efforts. These tools help with keyword research, site audits, performance tracking, and competitive analysis. Some essential SEO tools include:

- **Google Analytics:** Provides insights into website traffic, user behavior, and conversion tracking.
- **Google Search Console:** Offers data on search performance, indexing status, and technical issues.
- **SEMrush:** A comprehensive tool for keyword research, competitor analysis, and site audits.
- **Ahrefs:** Known for its backlink analysis capabilities, keyword research, and content exploration.
- **Moz Pro:** Offers keyword research, link building, and site audit features.

- **Yoast SEO (for WordPress):** A plugin that helps optimize WordPress sites for SEO with on-page suggestions and readability analysis.

- **Screaming Frog SEO Spider:** A tool for conducting in-depth technical site audits to identify and fix SEO issues.

By leveraging these tools, businesses can enhance their SEO strategies, monitor performance, and make data-driven decisions to improve their search engine rankings and achieve online success.

Chapter 4: The best way to do Content Marketing in modern times

Importance of High-Quality Content

High-quality content is the cornerstone of any successful digital marketing strategy. It serves multiple purposes: attracting and engaging your target audience, establishing your brand's authority and credibility, driving organic traffic through search engine optimization (SEO), and converting visitors into customers. Quality content resonates with readers, providing them with valuable information that addresses their needs and pain points. This, in turn, fosters trust and loyalty, encouraging repeat visits and long-term customer relationships.

Content that is well-researched, informative, and engaging can significantly enhance your brand's visibility and reputation. It helps in building a connection with your audience, which is crucial in today's competitive digital landscape. Moreover, high-quality content is more likely to be shared across social media platforms, amplifying your reach and driving more traffic to your site.

Developing a Content Strategy

Creating a robust content strategy involves several key steps:

1. **Define Your Goals:** Start by identifying what you want to achieve with your content marketing efforts.

This could be increasing brand awareness, generating leads, driving traffic, or boosting sales.

2. **Understand Your Audience:** Conduct thorough research to understand your target audience's demographics, interests, and pain points. This will help you create content that resonates with them.

3. **Perform a Content Audit:** Evaluate your existing content to identify gaps and opportunities. Determine what types of content have performed well and what needs improvement.

4. **Create a Content Plan:** Develop a content calendar that outlines what type of content you will create, when you will publish it, and on which platforms. This plan should align with your overall marketing goals and consider seasonal trends and events.

5. **Develop Content:** Based on your plan, start creating high-quality content. Ensure that each piece is well-researched, informative, and engaging. Use a mix of formats to cater to different preferences within your audience.

6. **Optimize for SEO:** Incorporate relevant keywords naturally into your content to improve its visibility in search engine results. Ensure that your content is well-structured, with clear headings and subheadings.

7. **Distribute and Promote:** Share your content across various channels, including your website, social media platforms, email newsletters, and third-party websites. Use paid promotion if necessary to reach a broader audience.

8. **Analyze and Adjust:** Regularly review your content's performance using analytics tools. Track key metrics such as traffic, engagement, and conversions. Use this data to refine your strategy and improve future content.

Types of Content (Blogs, Videos, Infographics, etc.)

Diverse content types cater to different audience preferences and help in keeping your content strategy dynamic and engaging. Here are some common types of content:

1. **Blogs:** Blog posts are an excellent way to share in-depth information, provide insights, and establish your expertise in a particular niche. They are also beneficial for SEO, as they can target a wide range of keywords.

2. **Videos:** Videos are highly engaging and can convey complex information in an easily digestible format. They are great for tutorials, product demonstrations, and storytelling.

3. **Infographics:** Infographics are visual representations of data and information. They are perfect for simplifying complex topics and making them more accessible and shareable.

4. **eBooks:** eBooks offer detailed information on a specific topic and are often used as lead magnets to capture email addresses.

5. **Podcasts:** Podcasts are an excellent way to reach audiences who prefer listening over reading. They

can cover a wide range of topics, from interviews to discussions on industry trends.

6. **Social Media Posts:** Short, engaging posts on platforms like Facebook, Twitter, and Instagram can help drive traffic to your site and increase brand awareness.

7. **Webinars:** Webinars are interactive sessions that allow you to engage with your audience in real-time. They are ideal for educating your audience and generating leads.

8. **Case Studies:** Case studies provide real-life examples of how your products or services have helped clients. They are effective for building credibility and trust.

Content Distribution Channels

Effectively distributing your content ensures it reaches the right audience. Here are some primary distribution channels:

1. **Website:** Your website is the central hub for your content. Ensure it's well-organized and optimized for SEO to attract organic traffic.

2. **Social Media:** Platforms like Facebook, Twitter, LinkedIn, and Instagram are excellent for promoting your content and engaging with your audience.

3. **Email Marketing:** Sending regular newsletters with your latest content helps keep your audience informed and engaged.

4. **Content Syndication:** Syndicate your content on third-party websites to reach a broader audience and drive more traffic to your site.

5. **Paid Promotion:** Use paid advertising on social media platforms and search engines to boost your content's visibility.

6. **Influencer Partnerships:** Collaborate with influencers to promote your content to their followers, increasing your reach and credibility.

7. **Online Communities and Forums:** Share your content in relevant online communities and forums to engage with niche audiences.

8. **Guest Blogging:** Write articles for other reputable websites in your industry to gain exposure and backlinks.

By leveraging these distribution channels, you can ensure your content reaches a wider audience, driving more traffic and achieving your marketing goals.

Chapter 5: The best way to do Social Media Marketing in modern times

Selecting the Right Social Media Platforms

Choosing the right social media platforms is crucial for the success of your social media marketing strategy. Not all platforms are created equal, and each has its own unique audience and best practices.

5 steps to help you select the right platforms:

1. **Identify Your Target Audience:**
    - Understand who your ideal customers are by analyzing demographics, interests, and behaviors. Tools like Google Analytics and social media insights can provide valuable data.

2. **Analyze Platform Demographics:**
    - Research the user demographics of different social media platforms. For example, LinkedIn is more business-oriented and popular among professionals, while

Instagram attracts a younger audience interested in visual content.

3. **Consider Your Content Type:**
   - Different platforms support different types of content. Instagram and Pinterest are ideal for visual content, while Twitter and LinkedIn are better for text-based updates and professional content. YouTube is perfect for video content.

4. **Evaluate Platform Features:**
   - Each platform offers unique features that can enhance your marketing efforts. For instance, Instagram Stories and Reels can boost engagement, while LinkedIn's job postings can help with recruitment.

5. **Assess Your Resources:**
   - Determine the resources you have available, such as time, budget, and staff. Managing multiple platforms can be time-consuming, so focus on the ones that offer the best ROI for your efforts.

By carefully selecting the platforms that align with your audience and content type, you can maximize your social media marketing effectiveness [3].

Creating Engaging Social Media Content

Creating engaging content is key to capturing and retaining your audience's attention on social media. Here are some strategies to create content that resonates:

1. **Know Your Audience:**
   - Create content that addresses the interests, needs, and pain points of your target audience. Use insights from social media analytics to understand what types of content perform best.

2. **Use High-Quality Visuals:**
   - Invest in high-quality images, videos, and graphics. Visual content is more likely to be shared and can significantly increase engagement.

3. **Tell Stories:**
   - Use storytelling to make your content more relatable and memorable. Share behind-the-scenes looks, customer testimonials, and brand stories to build a connection with your audience.

4. **Be Consistent:**
   - Maintain a consistent posting schedule to keep your audience engaged. Use a content calendar to plan and schedule posts in advance.

5. **Encourage Interaction:**
   - Ask questions, run polls, and encourage user-generated content. Engaging with your audience can increase visibility and foster a sense of community.

6. **Leverage Trends:**

- Stay up-to-date with the latest trends and incorporate them into your content. Use trending hashtags, participate in viral challenges, and create content around current events to increase reach.

By creating content that is engaging, visually appealing, and relevant to your audience, you can build a strong social media presence and foster meaningful interactions [4].

Social Media Advertising Strategies

Paid social media advertising can amplify your reach and help you achieve specific marketing goals. Here are some effective strategies:

1. **Define Your Objectives:**
   - Set clear objectives for your social media advertising campaigns, such as increasing brand awareness, generating leads, or driving sales.

2. **Target Your Audience:**
   - Use the advanced targeting options available on social media platforms to reach your ideal audience. Target based on demographics, interests, behaviors, and more.

3. **Choose the Right Ad Formats:**
   - Select the ad formats that best suit your objectives and content. Options include image ads, video ads, carousel ads, and sponsored posts.

4. **Create Compelling Ad Content:**

- Design visually appealing ads with clear, concise messaging. Use strong calls-to-action (CTAs) to encourage users to take the desired action.

5. **Set a Budget and Bidding Strategy:**
   - Determine your budget and choose a bidding strategy that aligns with your objectives. Platforms like Facebook and Instagram offer various bidding options, such as cost-per-click (CPC) and cost-per-impression (CPM).

6. **Monitor and Optimize:**
   - Regularly monitor the performance of your ads using analytics tools. Adjust your targeting, creative, and bidding strategy based on performance data to optimize results.

By implementing these strategies, you can effectively leverage social media advertising to achieve your marketing goals and maximize ROI [2].

Tools for Social Media Management

Managing social media accounts efficiently requires the right tools. Here are some essential tools for social media management:

1. **Hootsuite:**
   - Hootsuite allows you to schedule posts, monitor social media activity, and analyze performance across multiple platforms from a single dashboard.

2. **Buffer:**
    - Buffer helps you plan, schedule, and publish content. It also provides analytics to measure the effectiveness of your social media campaigns.

3. **Sprout Social:**
    - Sprout Social offers social media management, analytics, and engagement tools. It helps you understand your audience and improve your social media strategy.

4. **Canva:**
    - Canva is a design tool that enables you to create stunning visuals for your social media posts, including images, infographics, and videos [3].

5. **Later:**
    - Later focuses on visual content planning and scheduling, particularly for Instagram. It provides a visual content calendar and analytics.

6. **BuzzSumo:**
    - BuzzSumo helps you discover trending topics and content ideas. It also allows you to analyze your competitors and identify key influencers in your industry.

By using these tools, you can streamline your social media management, create engaging content, and analyze performance to improve your social media marketing efforts

Chapter 6: The best way to do Email Marketing in modern times

Building an Email List

An effective email marketing strategy begins with building a robust and engaged email list. Your email list is the foundation of your email marketing efforts, and growing it with quality subscribers is crucial.

7 key steps to build a successful email list:

1. **Create Compelling Sign-Up Forms:**
   - Design attractive and user-friendly sign-up forms. Use clear and concise language to explain the benefits of subscribing.
   - Place sign-up forms strategically on your website, such as on the homepage, blog posts, and landing pages.

2. **Offer Incentives:**
   - Provide valuable incentives to encourage people to subscribe to your email list. This could be in the form of discounts, free eBooks, exclusive content, or access to webinars.

- Clearly communicate the value of these incentives to potential subscribers.

3. **Leverage Social Media:**
   - Use your social media platforms to promote your email list. Share links to your sign-up forms and highlight the benefits of subscribing.
   - Run social media campaigns and contests that require participants to join your email list.

4. **Optimize for Mobile:**
   - Ensure that your sign-up forms are mobile-friendly. A significant portion of users access the internet through mobile devices, and a seamless mobile experience can boost your sign-up rates.

5. **Segment Your Audience:**
   - From the beginning, segment your audience based on interests, behaviors, or demographics. This allows you to send more targeted and relevant emails, increasing engagement and reducing unsubscribes.

6. **Use Pop-Ups and Slide-Ins:**
   - Implement pop-ups and slide-ins on your website to capture visitors' attention and encourage them to subscribe. Use timing and triggers, such as exit-intent, to maximize effectiveness without being intrusive.

7. **Ensure Compliance:**
   - Follow email marketing regulations, such as the GDPR and CAN-SPAM Act. Obtain explicit consent from subscribers and provide clear options for opting out.

Crafting Effective Email Campaigns

Creating engaging and effective email campaigns requires a thoughtful approach and attention to detail.

6 essential components of successful email campaigns:

1. **Personalization:**
   - Personalize your emails by addressing subscribers by their first name and tailoring content based on their preferences and behaviors.
   - Use dynamic content to show different messages to different segments of your audience.

2. **Compelling Subject Lines:**
   - Write attention-grabbing subject lines that entice subscribers to open your emails. Keep them short, relevant, and create a sense of urgency or curiosity.

3. **Engaging Content:**
   - Provide valuable and relevant content that addresses your subscribers' needs and interests. Mix different types of content, such

as articles, videos, and infographics, to keep your emails engaging.
- Ensure your emails are well-structured with a clear hierarchy, making it easy for readers to scan and find key information.

4. **Strong Call-to-Actions (CTAs):**
   - Include clear and compelling CTAs that guide subscribers towards the desired action, such as making a purchase, downloading a resource, or registering for an event.
   - Use actionable language and ensure your CTAs stand out visually.

5. **Responsive Design:**
   - Design your emails to be responsive and look great on all devices, including desktops, tablets, and smartphones. Test your emails on various devices to ensure they render correctly.

6. **A/B Testing:**
   - Conduct A/B testing to compare different elements of your emails, such as subject lines, content, and CTAs. Use the insights gained to optimize future campaigns.

Analyzing Email Marketing Metrics

Tracking and analyzing email marketing metrics is crucial for understanding the performance of your campaigns and making data-driven decisions.

7 key metrics to monitor:

1. **Open Rate:**
   - The percentage of recipients who open your email. A high open rate indicates that your subject lines are effective and your audience is engaged.

2. **Click-Through Rate (CTR):**
   - The percentage of recipients who click on a link within your email. CTR helps measure the effectiveness of your content and CTAs.

3. **Conversion Rate:**
   - The percentage of recipients who complete the desired action after clicking on a link in your email. This could be making a purchase, filling out a form, or downloading a resource.

4. **Bounce Rate:**
   - The percentage of emails that could not be delivered to recipients' inboxes. A high bounce rate can indicate issues with your email list quality or deliverability.

5. **Unsubscribe Rate:**
   - The percentage of recipients who unsubscribe from your email list after receiving an email. Monitoring this metric helps identify if your content is resonating with your audience.

6. **List Growth Rate:**

- The rate at which your email list is growing. A healthy list growth rate indicates successful list-building strategies and audience engagement.

7. **Email Sharing/Forwarding Rate:**
    - The percentage of recipients who share or forward your email to others. High sharing rates can expand your reach and attract new subscribers.

Tools for Email Marketing

Several tools can help streamline your email marketing efforts and enhance the effectiveness of your campaigns.

6 popular email marketing tools:

1. **Mailchimp:**
    - Mailchimp is a widely used email marketing platform that offers features for list building, email creation, automation, and analytics. It is suitable for businesses of all sizes.

2. **Constant Contact:**
    - Constant Contact provides easy-to-use tools for email creation, list management, and automation. It also offers event marketing and social media integration features.

3. **HubSpot:**
    - HubSpot's email marketing software integrates with its CRM, allowing for personalized and automated email

campaigns. It offers robust analytics and segmentation capabilities.

4. **Sendinblue:**
    - Sendinblue offers email marketing, SMS marketing, and automation features. It is known for its user-friendly interface and affordability.

5. **ActiveCampaign:**
    - ActiveCampaign combines email marketing with powerful automation and CRM features. It is ideal for businesses looking to create complex automated workflows.

6. **AWeber:**
    - AWeber provides email marketing and automation tools with a focus on simplicity and ease of use. It offers a range of templates and integrates with various third-party apps.

By utilizing these tools, you can efficiently manage your email marketing campaigns, create engaging content, and analyze performance to continually improve your strategies.

Chapter 7: Pay-Per-Click (PPC) Advertising

Introduction to PPC

Pay-Per-Click (PPC) advertising is a digital marketing model where advertisers pay a fee each time their ad is clicked. It is a way of buying visits to your site rather than attempting to earn those visits organically. PPC ads can appear on search engines, social media platforms, and other websites, providing businesses with a powerful tool to drive traffic, generate leads, and increase sales.

PPC is highly effective because it targets users who are actively searching for specific products or services, making them more likely to convert. The most common form of PPC is search engine advertising, where advertisers bid for ad placement in a search engine's sponsored links when someone searches for a keyword related to their business [2].

Creating Effective PPC Campaigns

6 key steps to creating a successful PPC campaign:

1. **Keyword Research:**
    - Identify relevant keywords that potential customers are likely to use when searching for your products or services. Use tools like

Google Keyword Planner, Ahrefs, and SEMrush to find high-traffic, low-competition keywords.

2. **Ad Creation:**
   - Write compelling ad copy that includes your target keywords. Ensure your ads are clear, concise, and include a strong call to action (CTA). Use ad extensions to provide additional information, such as links to specific pages on your website, your phone number, or your business location.

3. **Landing Page Optimization:**
   - Direct users to a landing page that is relevant to the ad and optimized for conversions. Ensure the landing page is user-friendly, has a clear CTA, and provides all necessary information to encourage visitors to take action.

4. **Bid Management:**
   - Set a budget for your PPC campaigns and determine how much you are willing to pay for each click. Use automated bidding strategies offered by platforms like Google Ads to optimize your bids based on your campaign goals.

5. **Targeting:**
   - Use advanced targeting options to reach your ideal audience. This includes geographic targeting, demographic targeting, and

behavioral targeting. Refine your targeting based on the performance data to maximize the effectiveness of your campaigns.

6. **Monitoring and Adjusting:**
    - Regularly monitor the performance of your PPC campaigns using analytics tools. Track key metrics such as click-through rate (CTR), conversion rate, cost-per-click (CPC), and return on ad spend (ROAS). Make data-driven adjustments to your keywords, ad copy, bids, and targeting to improve performance [1].

Analyzing PPC Performance

Analyzing the performance of your PPC campaigns is crucial for optimizing your strategy and maximizing ROI.

7 key metrics to track:

1. **Click-Through Rate (CTR):**
    - CTR measures the number of clicks your ad receives divided by the number of times your ad is shown (impressions). A high CTR indicates that your ad is relevant and appealing to users.

2. **Conversion Rate:**
    - Conversion rate is the percentage of users who take the desired action (e.g., making a purchase, filling out a form) after clicking on your ad. This metric helps you assess the

effectiveness of your landing page and overall campaign.

3. **Cost-Per-Click (CPC):**
    - CPC is the amount you pay for each click on your ad. Monitoring CPC helps you manage your budget and ensure that your campaigns are cost-effective.

4. **Quality Score:**
    - Quality Score is a metric used by Google Ads that measures the relevance and quality of your keywords and ads. A higher Quality Score can lead to lower CPCs and better ad positions.

5. **Return on Ad Spend (ROAS):**
    - ROAS measures the revenue generated from your PPC campaigns compared to the amount spent on the ads. A high ROAS indicates a profitable campaign.

6. **Impression Share:**
    - Impression share is the percentage of times your ads were shown out of the total available impressions. It helps you understand your ad visibility and identify opportunities for improvement.

7. **Bounce Rate:**
    - Bounce rate is the percentage of visitors who leave your site after viewing only one page. A high bounce rate may indicate that your

landing page is not relevant or engaging enough.

By regularly analyzing these metrics, you can gain insights into what's working and what needs improvement, allowing you to optimize your PPC campaigns for better performance and higher ROI [5].

Tools for PPC Management

Several tools can help streamline your PPC management and enhance the effectiveness of your campaigns.

7 essential PPC management tools:

1. **Google Ads:**
   - Google Ads is the most popular PPC platform, offering a wide range of features for creating, managing, and optimizing PPC campaigns. It provides detailed analytics and automated bidding strategies to help you achieve your goals.

2. **Microsoft Advertising:**
   - Microsoft Advertising (formerly Bing Ads) allows you to reach a different segment of search engine users. It offers similar features to Google Ads and can be a valuable addition to your PPC strategy.

3. **SEMrush:**
   - SEMrush is a comprehensive tool that provides keyword research, competitive analysis, and PPC campaign management. It helps you find profitable keywords, track

your competitors, and optimize your ad performance.

4. **Ahrefs:**
    - Ahrefs is known for its robust keyword research and competitive analysis capabilities. It can help you identify high-performing keywords and analyze your competitors' PPC strategies.

5. **WordStream:**
    - WordStream offers a suite of tools for managing and optimizing PPC campaigns across multiple platforms. Its 20-Minute Work Week feature provides actionable recommendations to improve your campaigns quickly.

6. **SpyFu:**
    - SpyFu allows you to analyze your competitors' PPC campaigns, including their keywords, ad copy, and performance metrics. This insight can help you refine your own strategies and stay competitive.

7. **Optmyzr:**
    - Optmyzr provides advanced PPC management tools, including automated optimization, bid management, and performance tracking. It integrates with multiple PPC platforms, making it easy to manage your campaigns in one place.

By leveraging these tools, you can efficiently manage your PPC campaigns, optimize your ad performance, and achieve your marketing goals

Chapter 8: Analytics and Data-Driven Marketing

Importance of Data in Digital Marketing

Data is the backbone of effective digital marketing strategies. It enables marketers to understand their audience, track campaign performance, and make informed decisions that drive results.

4 reasons why data is crucial in digital marketing:

1. **Informed Decision Making:**
    - Data provides insights into customer behavior, preferences, and trends, allowing marketers to make evidence-based decisions rather than relying on intuition or guesswork [2].
2. **Personalization:**
    - By analyzing data, marketers can create personalized experiences for customers. Personalization enhances customer engagement and satisfaction by delivering relevant content and offers [4].
3. **Optimization:**

- Continuous data analysis helps optimize marketing strategies and tactics. Marketers can identify what works and what doesn't, making necessary adjustments to improve performance [1].

4. **ROI Measurement:**
   - Data allows marketers to measure the return on investment (ROI) of their campaigns. By tracking key performance indicators (KPIs), they can assess the effectiveness of their marketing efforts and allocate resources efficiently [3].

Tools for Data Collection and Analysis

Effective data-driven marketing relies on robust tools for data collection and analysis.

5 essential tools:

1. **Google Analytics:**
   - A powerful tool that provides insights into website traffic, user behavior, and conversion rates. It helps marketers understand how visitors interact with their site and which channels drive the most traffic.

2. **SEMrush:**
   - A comprehensive tool for keyword research, competitive analysis, and tracking SEO performance. It provides valuable data on search trends, backlinks, and content marketing effectiveness [4].

3. **HubSpot:**
   - An all-in-one marketing platform that includes tools for email marketing, social media management, and customer relationship management (CRM). It offers detailed analytics and reporting features.

4. **Tableau:**
   - A data visualization tool that helps marketers create interactive and shareable dashboards. It enables easy exploration of large datasets and provides clear insights through visual representation.

5. **Hotjar:**
   - A tool for analyzing user behavior on websites through heatmaps, session recordings, and surveys. It helps marketers understand how users interact with their site and identify areas for improvement.

Making Data-Driven Decisions

Data-driven decision-making involves using data to guide strategic and tactical marketing choices.

5 ways to implement it:

1. **Define Objectives:**
   - Start by setting clear marketing objectives that align with your business goals. Objectives could include increasing website traffic, improving conversion rates, or boosting customer retention.

2. **Collect Relevant Data:**
   - Use the tools mentioned above to gather data on key metrics. Ensure the data collected is relevant to your objectives and provides actionable insights.

3. **Analyze Data:**
   - Analyze the collected data to identify patterns, trends, and correlations. Use statistical methods and data visualization tools to make sense of the data and derive insights.

4. **Formulate Strategies:**
   - Based on the insights gained, develop marketing strategies that address the identified opportunities and challenges. Ensure that your strategies are backed by data and have measurable goals.

5. **Implement and Monitor:**
    - Execute your strategies and continuously monitor their performance using real-time data. Make adjustments as needed to optimize outcomes.

6. **Review and Optimize:**
    - Regularly review the results of your marketing efforts. Use the insights from your analysis to refine your strategies and improve future performance [6].

7 Key Metrics to Track

Tracking the right metrics is essential for evaluating the success of your digital marketing efforts. Here are some key metrics to focus on:

1. **Website Traffic:**
    - Monitor the number of visitors to your website, their source, and their behavior. This includes metrics like page views, unique visitors, and bounce rate.

2. **Conversion Rate:**
    - The percentage of visitors who complete a desired action, such as making a purchase or filling out a form. This metric helps assess the effectiveness of your website and marketing campaigns.

3. **Cost Per Acquisition (CPA):**
   - The average cost to acquire a new customer. This metric helps evaluate the efficiency of your marketing spend.

4. **Customer Lifetime Value (CLV):**
   - The total revenue a business can expect from a single customer account. This metric helps in understanding the long-term value of your customers.

5. **Return on Investment (ROI):**
   - The measure of the profitability of your marketing efforts. ROI is calculated by dividing the net profit from your marketing activities by the total cost.

6. **Engagement Metrics:**
   - Track how users interact with your content across different channels. This includes metrics like likes, shares, comments, and time spent on page.

7. **Click-Through Rate (CTR):**
   - The percentage of people who click on a link or ad compared to the number of people who viewed it. CTR is crucial for evaluating the effectiveness of your ads and emails.

By focusing on these key metrics, you can gain a comprehensive understanding of your marketing performance and make data-driven decisions to improve your strategies [5].

Chapter 9: Trends and Innovations in Digital Marketing

The Role of Artificial Intelligence in Marketing

Artificial Intelligence (AI) has become a transformative force in digital marketing, offering new opportunities for efficiency, personalization, and data-driven decision-making. AI can analyze vast amounts of data at unprecedented speeds, providing insights that drive smarter marketing strategies.

5 key roles AI plays in marketing:

1. **Data Analysis and Insights:**
   - AI processes large volumes of data from various sources, including social media, emails, and web interactions. This allows marketers to gain deeper insights into consumer behavior and preferences [2].

2. **Personalization:**
   - AI enables personalized marketing by analyzing user data to deliver tailored content, product recommendations, and

advertisements. This enhances user experience and increases engagement [1].

3. **Chatbots and Customer Service:**

    o   AI-powered chatbots provide instant customer support, answering queries and resolving issues in real-time. This improves customer satisfaction and reduces the workload on human customer service representatives [4].

4. **Predictive Analytics:**

    o   AI uses predictive analytics to forecast trends and consumer behavior, helping marketers to anticipate needs and plan more effective campaigns [3].

5. **Content Creation:**

    o   AI tools can generate content, such as social media posts, blog articles, and email newsletters, based on predefined criteria and audience data. This speeds up the content creation process and ensures relevance [6].

Voice Search and Its Impact

Voice search is rapidly changing the way consumers interact with technology and search for information online. The rise of smart speakers and virtual assistants, such as Amazon's Alexa, Google Assistant, and Apple's Siri, has made voice search a critical component of digital marketing strategies.

1. **SEO for Voice Search:**

- Voice search queries are typically longer and more conversational than text searches. Marketers need to optimize their content for natural language and question-based queries to improve visibility in voice search results.

2. **Local SEO:**
    - Many voice searches are location-specific, such as finding nearby businesses or services. Optimizing for local SEO by including location-based keywords and maintaining accurate business listings is essential.

3. **Featured Snippets:**
    - Voice assistants often read out featured snippets from search results. Ensuring your content is structured to appear as a featured snippet can significantly increase your visibility in voice search.

4. **User Experience:**
    - Providing concise and direct answers to common questions improves the user experience for voice search users. This requires a focus on clear and informative content [5].

The Rise of Video Marketing

Video marketing has become one of the most effective ways to engage audiences and convey information. With the growth of platforms like YouTube, TikTok, and Instagram Reels, video content is more accessible and influential than ever.

1. **Increased Engagement:**
    - Videos capture attention better than text or images, leading to higher engagement rates. They are more likely to be shared on social media, increasing reach and visibility.

2. **Educational Content:**
    - Tutorials, product demos, and how-to videos provide valuable information to consumers, helping them make informed decisions and increasing brand trust.

3. **Live Streaming:**
    - Live streaming allows brands to interact with their audience in real-time, fostering a sense of community and immediacy. It is effective for product launches, Q&A sessions, and behind-the-scenes content.

4. **Storytelling:**
    - Videos are a powerful medium for storytelling, allowing brands to convey their message and values in an engaging way. Authentic and relatable stories can create a

strong emotional connection with the audience [4].

Emerging Social Media Platforms

As digital marketing evolves, new social media platforms continue to emerge, offering fresh opportunities for brands to connect with their audience. Staying ahead of trends and leveraging these platforms can provide a competitive advantage.

1. **TikTok:**
    - Known for its short, engaging videos, TikTok has quickly become a favorite among younger audiences. Brands can create viral content, participate in trending challenges, and collaborate with influencers to reach a broader audience.

2. **Clubhouse:**
    - An audio-based social networking app, Clubhouse allows users to join live discussions on various topics. Brands can host rooms, engage in conversations, and build thought leadership.

3. **Twitch:**
    - Originally a platform for gamers, Twitch has expanded to include content on music, art, and lifestyle. Brands can sponsor streams, collaborate with popular streamers, and create interactive experiences for viewers.

4. **Discord:**
   - Initially designed for gaming communities, Discord is now used by various interest groups. Brands can create servers to foster community engagement, provide customer support, and host events.
5. **Vero:**
   - A social media platform focused on authentic sharing, Vero allows users to share photos, music, books, and more without ads or algorithms. It appeals to users seeking a more genuine social media experience.

By embracing these emerging platforms, brands can stay relevant and engage with audiences in innovative ways [5].

Chapter 10: Creating an Integrated Digital Marketing Strategy

Combining Various Digital Marketing Tactics

An integrated digital marketing strategy combines multiple digital marketing tactics to create a cohesive and synergistic approach that drives business growth and enhances customer engagement.

6 ways effectively combine various digital marketing tactics:

1. **Content Marketing:**
   - Develop high-quality content that addresses the needs and interests of your target audience. This includes blog posts, articles, videos, infographics, and eBooks. Content marketing builds brand authority and drives organic traffic to your website [3].

2. **Search Engine Optimization (SEO):**
   - Optimize your website and content for search engines to improve visibility and attract organic traffic. Focus on keyword research,

on-page SEO, technical SEO, and link-building strategies [6].

3. **Social Media Marketing:**
    - Leverage social media platforms to connect with your audience, share content, and engage in conversations. Use a mix of organic and paid strategies to expand your reach and drive traffic to your website [5].

4. **Email Marketing:**
    - Build and nurture an email list to communicate directly with your audience. Use personalized and segmented email campaigns to deliver targeted messages that drive conversions and build customer loyalty [2].

5. **Pay-Per-Click (PPC) Advertising:**
    - Use PPC advertising to drive immediate traffic to your website. Platforms like Google Ads and social media ads allow you to target specific demographics and measure campaign performance in real-time [4].

6. **Affiliate Marketing:**
    - Partner with affiliates who promote your products or services in exchange for a commission. This expands your reach and leverages the influence of affiliates to drive sales [1].

Case Studies of Successful Digital Marketing Campaigns

Examining successful digital marketing campaigns provides valuable insights into what works and why.

3 case studies:

1. **Nike's "Just Do It" Campaign:**
   - Nike's iconic campaign used motivational messaging and high-profile athlete endorsements to connect with a broad audience. The campaign's success was driven by consistent branding, emotional appeal, and effective use of social media and influencer marketing [6].

2. **Coca-Cola's "Share a Coke" Campaign:**
   - This campaign personalized Coke bottles with people's names, encouraging customers to share photos on social media. The campaign's interactive and personal approach led to increased brand engagement and sales [3].

3. **Dove's "Real Beauty" Campaign:**
   - Dove's campaign focused on body positivity and self-esteem, featuring real women instead of models. The campaign's authenticity and alignment with brand values resonated with consumers, driving brand loyalty and social media buzz [4].

Creating a Long-Term Digital Marketing Plan

A long-term digital marketing plan ensures sustained growth and adaptation to changing market conditions. Here's how to create one:

1. **Set Clear Goals:**
   - Define specific, measurable, achievable, relevant, and time-bound (SMART) goals for your digital marketing efforts. These goals should align with your overall business objectives [5].

2. **Conduct a Situational Analysis:**
   - Analyze your current digital marketing performance, competitor strategies, and market trends. Use tools like SWOT analysis to identify strengths, weaknesses, opportunities, and threats [1].

3. **Develop a Strategy:**
   - Based on your analysis, create a strategy that outlines the tactics you will use to achieve your goals. This includes your content strategy, SEO plan, social media approach, and more [6].

4. **Implement and Execute:**
   - Put your plan into action by creating and distributing content, launching campaigns, and engaging with your audience. Ensure all

team members understand their roles and responsibilities [4].

5. **Monitor and Measure:**
    - Regularly track your performance using analytics tools. Monitor key metrics like traffic, engagement, conversion rates, and ROI to assess the effectiveness of your strategy [2].

6. **Adjust and Optimize:**
    - Use the insights gained from your performance data to make adjustments to your strategy. Continuously optimize your tactics to improve results and adapt to changes in the digital landscape [3].

Measuring and Adjusting Your Strategy

Effective measurement and adjustment are crucial for a successful digital marketing strategy.

5 ways to do it:

1. **Identify Key Metrics:**
    - Determine the key performance indicators (KPIs) that align with your goals. These might include website traffic, conversion rates, click-through rates, engagement metrics, and customer acquisition costs [6].
2. **Use Analytics Tools:**

- Utilize tools like Google Analytics, SEMrush, and social media analytics to gather data on your digital marketing activities. These tools provide insights into user behavior, campaign performance, and ROI [3].

3. **Analyze Data:**
    - Regularly analyze your data to identify trends, strengths, and areas for improvement. Look for patterns in customer behavior and campaign performance that can inform your strategy [2].

4. **Make Data-Driven Decisions:**
    - Use your data analysis to make informed decisions about your digital marketing tactics. Adjust your strategy based on what's working and what's not, focusing on high-performing channels and content [5].

5. **Continuous Improvement:**
    - Digital marketing is an ongoing process. Continuously refine your approach, test new ideas, and stay updated with industry trends to keep your strategy effective and relevant [4].

By combining various digital marketing tactics, learning from successful campaigns, creating a comprehensive long-term plan, and continuously measuring and adjusting your strategy, you can build a powerful digital marketing strategy that drives sustained growth and engagement.

Chapter 11: The best way to do Facebook Marketing in modern times

7 Insider Secrets to Creating the Best Facebook Page for Your Small Business

1. Optimize Your Profile

Ensure your profile picture and cover photo are high-quality and represent your brand. Use your logo for the profile picture and a compelling image or video for the cover photo that showcases your products or services.

2. Complete Your About Section

Fill out your About section with essential information about your business, including contact details, location, and a brief description of what you offer. Include keywords relevant to your business to improve searchability.

3. Post High-Quality Content

Regularly post engaging and high-quality content that adds value to your audience. This can include blog posts, images, videos, infographics, and customer testimonials. Mix promotional content with educational and entertaining posts to keep your audience interested.

4. Use Facebook Insights

Leverage Facebook Insights to understand your audience better and track the performance of your posts. Use this data to refine your content strategy and post at times when your audience is most active.

5. Engage with Your Audience

Respond to comments, messages, and reviews promptly. Show appreciation for positive feedback and address any concerns or complaints professionally. Engaging with your audience builds trust and loyalty.

6. Run Facebook Ads

Utilize Facebook Ads to reach a broader audience. Target your ads based on demographics, interests, and behaviors to ensure they are seen by potential customers who are most likely to be interested in your products or services.

7. Host Contests and Giveaways

Increase engagement and attract new followers by hosting contests and giveaways. Encourage participants to like, share, and comment on your posts to enter. This not only boosts your visibility but also grows your follower base.

13 Common Mistakes to Avoid with Your Facebook Page

1. **Inconsistent Branding:** Ensure your branding is consistent across all your posts, images, and videos.

2. **Ignoring Analytics:** Regularly check Facebook Insights to understand what content works best.

3. **Over-Posting:** Avoid overwhelming your audience with too many posts. Quality over quantity is key.

4. **Ignoring Comments:** Engage with your audience by responding to comments and messages promptly.

5. **Not Using Visuals:** Posts with images or videos perform better than text-only posts.

6. **Lack of Call-to-Action:** Encourage your audience to take action with clear calls-to-action.

7. **Neglecting Mobile Users:** Ensure your content is mobile-friendly, as many users access Facebook via mobile devices.

8. **Using Poor-Quality Images:** High-quality visuals are crucial for maintaining a professional image.

9. **Not Posting Regularly:** Keep your audience engaged by posting regularly.

10. **Ignoring Negative Feedback:** Address negative feedback professionally and promptly.

11. **Not Utilizing Ads:** Boost your reach with targeted Facebook ads.

12. **Over-Promoting:** Balance promotional content with engaging and valuable posts.

13. **Lack of Planning:** Develop a content calendar to plan your posts ahead of time.

13 Proven Ways to Get Tons of Facebook Page Followers

1. **Optimize Your Page:** Ensure your page is fully optimized with complete information and keywords.

2. **Invite Friends:** Invite your friends to like your page.

3. **Promote on Other Social Platforms:** Share your Facebook page on other social media platforms.

4. **Use Hashtags:** Use relevant hashtags to increase the discoverability of your posts.

5. **Run Contests:** Host contests that require participants to like your page.

6. **Post Engaging Content:** Share content that resonates with your audience.

7. **Collaborate with Influencers:** Partner with influencers to reach a broader audience.

8. **Utilize Facebook Ads:** Run targeted ads to attract new followers.

9. **Share User-Generated Content:** Encourage followers to share their content on your page.

10. **Engage with Comments:** Respond to comments to increase engagement.

11. **Host Live Videos:** Use Facebook Live to engage with your audience in real-time.

12. **Share Behind-the-Scenes Content:** Give followers a glimpse behind the scenes of your business.

13. **Offer Exclusive Deals:** Provide exclusive offers to your Facebook followers.

11 Fast Answers to the Most Frequently Asked Questions about Facebook Pages

1. **How often should I post?**
    - Post at least 1-2 times per day to keep your audience engaged without overwhelming them.

2. **What type of content performs best?**
    - Visual content, such as images and videos, generally performs better than text-only posts.

3. **How can I increase engagement?**
    - Engage with your audience by responding to comments and messages, and encourage interaction with questions and polls.

4. **Should I use Facebook Ads?**

- Yes, Facebook Ads can help you reach a larger and more targeted audience.

5. **How do I handle negative comments?**
   - Address negative comments professionally and promptly, showing that you value customer feedback.

6. **What is the best time to post?**
   - Use Facebook Insights to determine when your audience is most active and schedule your posts accordingly.

7. **How can I get more likes on my page?**
   - Promote your page on other social media platforms, run contests, and use Facebook Ads to attract more likes.

8. **What should I include in my About section?**
   - Include essential information about your business, such as contact details, location, and a brief description of your products or services.

9. **Can I link my Facebook page to my website?**
   - Yes, add a Facebook link on your website and encourage visitors to follow your page.

10. **How do I measure the success of my posts?**

- Use Facebook Insights to track engagement metrics, such as likes, comments, shares, and reach.

11. **Should I use Facebook Live?**
    - Yes, Facebook Live is a great way to engage with your audience in real-time and build a personal connection.

Facebook Fan Page Quick Start Guide

1. **Create Your Page:**
    - Go to Facebook and click on "Create" to start setting up your business page.

2. **Add a Profile and Cover Photo:**
    - Use high-quality images that represent your brand.

3. **Fill Out the About Section:**
    - Provide essential information about your business, including contact details and a brief description.

4. **Post High-Quality Content:**
    - Share engaging content regularly to keep your audience interested.

5. **Promote Your Page:**

- Use Facebook Ads, invite friends, and share your page on other social media platforms.

6. **Engage with Your Audience:**
    - Respond to comments and messages promptly to build a loyal following.

7. **Analyze Your Performance:**
    - Use Facebook Insights to track the success of your posts and refine your strategy.

Facebook Pages Best Practices

1. **Consistency:** Maintain a consistent posting schedule.
2. **Visual Content:** Use high-quality images and videos.
3. **Engagement:** Respond to comments and messages.
4. **Promotion:** Use ads and cross-promotion to increase visibility.
5. **Analytics:** Regularly check Facebook Insights to understand your audience and improve your content strategy.

Next Steps

- Implement the strategies and tips provided in this chapter to optimize your Facebook marketing efforts.
- Continuously monitor your performance and adjust your strategy based on insights and feedback.

- Stay updated with the latest trends and best practices in Facebook marketing to maintain your competitive edge.

Recommended Resources

1. **Facebook for Business:** Facebook Business
2. **Hootsuite:** A social media management tool to help schedule posts and analyze performance.
3. **Canva:** A design tool to create stunning visuals for your Facebook page.
4. **Buffer:** Another social media management tool for scheduling posts and tracking performance.
5. **Sprout Social:** A comprehensive tool for social media management and analytics.

Chapter 12: The best way to do TikTok Marketing in modern times

Introduction to TikTok Marketing

TikTok has rapidly evolved from a platform for viral dance videos to a powerful marketing tool for businesses. With over a billion active users, it presents an unparalleled opportunity to reach a vast and engaged audience. This chapter will guide you through the essentials of TikTok marketing, providing strategies and tips to effectively promote your brand.

Creating Your TikTok Strategy

Understand Your Audience

Before diving into TikTok marketing, it's crucial to understand the platform's demographic. TikTok primarily attracts younger audiences, with a significant portion of users being Gen Z and millennials. Tailoring your content to resonate with these age groups will enhance engagement and effectiveness.

Set Clear Goals

Determine what you want to achieve with your TikTok marketing efforts. Whether it's brand awareness, driving website traffic, or increasing sales, having clear objectives will guide your content creation and marketing strategies.

Crafting Engaging Content

Leverage Trends and Challenges

One of TikTok's unique features is its trends and challenges, which often go viral. Participating in relevant trends and creating challenge-based content can boost your visibility and engagement. Ensure that your content aligns with your brand and adds value to the audience.

Create Authentic and Relatable Content

TikTok users value authenticity. Create content that feels genuine and relatable, avoiding overly polished and commercialized videos. Showcase behind-the-scenes glimpses, user-generated content, and real-life stories to build a connection with your audience.

Use Hashtags Strategically

Hashtags are essential for increasing the discoverability of your content. Use trending and relevant hashtags to reach a broader audience. Additionally, create a branded hashtag for your campaigns to encourage user participation and content creation.

Collaborating with Influencers

Identify the Right Influencers

Influencer marketing is highly effective on TikTok. Identify influencers whose audience aligns with your target demographic. Collaborate with them to create authentic and engaging content that promotes your brand.

Create Mutually Beneficial Partnerships

Work with influencers to develop campaigns that benefit both parties. Provide them with creative freedom to ensure the content feels natural and resonates with their followers.

Running TikTok Ads

Types of TikTok Ads

TikTok offers various ad formats, including In-Feed Ads, Branded Hashtag Challenges, Branded Effects, and TopView Ads. Each format has its advantages, so choose the one that best aligns with your marketing goals and budget.

Targeting Your Ads

Utilize TikTok's robust targeting options to reach your desired audience. You can target users based on demographics, interests, and behaviors, ensuring your ads are seen by those most likely to engage with your brand.

Measuring Success

Key Metrics to Track

Monitor metrics such as views, likes, shares, comments, and follower growth to gauge the performance of your TikTok marketing efforts. Additionally, track website traffic and conversions generated from your TikTok campaigns.

Using Analytics Tools

Leverage TikTok's built-in analytics tools to gain insights into your audience's behavior and preferences. Use this data to refine your content strategy and improve future campaigns.

Best Practices for TikTok Marketing

1. **Consistency:** Post regularly to keep your audience engaged and maintain visibility.

2. **Creativity:** Experiment with different content formats and ideas to see what resonates best with your audience.

3. **Engagement:** Respond to comments and messages to build a loyal community.

4. **Cross-Promotion:** Promote your TikTok content on other social media platforms to increase reach.

5. **Feedback:** Pay attention to feedback and adapt your strategy accordingly.

Conclusion

TikTok marketing offers a dynamic and exciting way to connect with a vast audience. By understanding the platform, creating engaging content, collaborating with influencers, and leveraging ads, you can effectively promote your brand on TikTok. Continuously monitor your performance and adapt your strategy to stay ahead in the ever-evolving digital landscape.

Chapter 13: The best way to do Instagram Marketing in modern times

Introduction

Instagram has become an essential platform for businesses aiming to reach a massive audience. With over a billion monthly active users, Instagram offers unparalleled opportunities to grow your brand and achieve significant follower milestones. This chapter will cover everything you need to know to grow your Instagram page to 1 million followers.

Optimize Your Profile

1. **Profile Picture and Bio**: Your profile picture should be a high-quality image that represents your brand, typically your logo. Your bio should be compelling and include relevant keywords, a clear description of your business, and a call to action with a link to your website or a landing page.

2. **Username and Handle**: Ensure your username is consistent with your other social media handles and easy to remember. This consistency helps with brand recognition.

Content Strategy

1. **Content Calendar**: Plan your posts in advance using a content calendar. This ensures a consistent posting schedule and helps maintain a balanced mix of content types (e.g., photos, videos, stories, IGTV).

2. **High-Quality Visuals**: Instagram is a visual platform, so invest in high-quality photos and videos. Use tools like Canva to create visually appealing content.

3. **Engaging Captions**: Write captions that resonate with your audience. Use a mix of storytelling, questions, and calls to action to encourage engagement.

Leveraging Instagram Features

1. **Stories**: Use Instagram Stories to share behind-the-scenes content, daily updates, and engage with your audience through polls, Q&A sessions, and interactive stickers.

2. **IGTV**: Create long-form videos that provide value to your audience. This could include tutorials, product demonstrations, or interviews.

3. **Reels**: Leverage Instagram Reels to reach a broader audience. Reels are short, engaging videos that can go viral quickly.

Hashtags and Geotags

1. **Effective Hashtag Strategy**: Use a mix of popular, niche, and branded hashtags to increase the

discoverability of your posts. Research and include up to 30 relevant hashtags per post.

2. **Geotags**: Tag your location to attract local followers and increase the reach of your posts.

Engagement Tactics

1. **Interact with Followers**: Respond to comments and messages promptly. Engage with your followers by liking and commenting on their posts.

2. **Collaborate with Influencers**: Partner with influencers who align with your brand to reach their followers. Influencer collaborations can significantly boost your visibility and follower count.

3. **User-Generated Content**: Encourage your followers to create content related to your brand. Share this user-generated content on your profile to build community and trust.

Instagram Ads

1. **Targeted Ads**: Use Instagram's advertising platform to run targeted ads. Define your audience based on demographics, interests, and behaviors to reach potential followers effectively.

2. **Ad Formats**: Experiment with different ad formats such as photo ads, video ads, carousel ads, and story ads to see what resonates best with your audience.

Analyzing Performance

1. **Instagram Insights**: Regularly review Instagram Insights to track the performance of your posts and

stories. Monitor metrics like reach, impressions, and engagement to understand what works best.

2. **Adjust Your Strategy**: Use the insights gathered to adjust your content strategy. Focus on creating more of the content that performs well and less of what doesn't.

Common Mistakes to Avoid

1. **Inconsistent Posting**: Maintain a consistent posting schedule to keep your audience engaged.

2. **Ignoring Analytics**: Regularly review your analytics to understand what content resonates with your audience.

3. **Neglecting Engagement**: Engage with your followers by responding to comments and messages promptly.

4. **Over-Promoting**: Balance promotional content with engaging and valuable posts to avoid turning off your audience.

Conclusion

Growing your Instagram page to 1 million followers requires a strategic approach, consistent effort, and a deep understanding of your audience. By optimizing your profile, creating high-quality content, leveraging Instagram's features, engaging with your audience, running targeted ads, and continuously analyzing your performance, you can achieve significant growth on this powerful platform.

Chapter 14: The best way to do YouTube Marketing in modern times

YouTube has emerged as a powerful platform for marketers, content creators, and businesses aiming to reach a vast audience. Growing a YouTube channel to one million followers is an ambitious but achievable goal with the right strategies and consistent effort. This chapter will cover everything you need to know to turn your YouTube channel into a thriving hub with a massive following.

Creating Compelling Content

Know Your Audience

Understanding your target audience is crucial. Identify their interests, problems, and the type of content they engage with. Use YouTube Analytics to gain insights into your viewers' demographics and behaviors.

Content Planning

Develop a content calendar to ensure consistency. Plan your videos around trending topics, seasonal events, and viewer preferences. Mix up your content with tutorials, vlogs, interviews, and behind-the-scenes footage to keep your audience engaged.

Quality Over Quantity

Focus on producing high-quality content. Invest in good camera equipment, lighting, and sound. Well-edited videos with clear audio and visual appeal will attract and retain viewers.

Thumbnails and Titles

Create eye-catching thumbnails and compelling titles. Thumbnails should be vibrant and relevant to the video content, while titles should be descriptive and keyword-rich to improve discoverability.

Optimizing Your Channel

Channel Branding

Your channel should reflect your brand's identity. Use a consistent logo, color scheme, and tone across your channel art, thumbnails, and video content.

About Section

Optimize your channel's About section with relevant keywords and a concise description of what your channel offers. Include links to your website and social media profiles.

Playlists

Organize your videos into playlists based on themes or series. Playlists encourage binge-watching, which increases your channel's watch time and helps in ranking.

Tags and Descriptions

Use relevant tags and detailed descriptions for each video. This helps YouTube's algorithm understand your content and recommend it to the right audience.

Engaging with Your Audience

Comments and Feedback

Engage with your viewers by responding to comments and asking for feedback. Building a community around your channel fosters loyalty and encourages viewers to share your content.

Community Tab

Utilize the Community tab to post updates, polls, and behind-the-scenes content. This keeps your audience engaged between video uploads.

Live Streaming

Host live streams to interact with your audience in real-time. Live streams can boost your channel's engagement and provide an opportunity to answer viewer questions directly.

Promoting Your Channel

Collaborations

Collaborate with other YouTubers in your niche. This exposes your channel to a broader audience and can lead to cross-promotion opportunities.

Social Media Promotion

Promote your videos on all your social media platforms. Use teaser clips, behind-the-scenes content, and links to drive traffic from social media to your YouTube channel.

SEO Strategies

Optimize your videos for search engines by including keywords in your titles, descriptions, and tags. Use YouTube Analytics to track the performance of your SEO efforts and adjust your strategy accordingly.

Advertisements

Invest in YouTube Ads to reach a larger audience. Use targeted ads to promote your channel and specific videos to users who are likely to be interested in your content.

Analyzing and Adjusting

YouTube Analytics

Regularly check YouTube Analytics to monitor your channel's performance. Track metrics such as watch time, audience retention, and click-through rates to understand what works and what doesn't.

Adjusting Content Strategy

Based on your analytics, adjust your content strategy to align with viewer preferences. Experiment with different types of content and posting times to see what resonates best with your audience.

Continuous Improvement

Stay updated with the latest YouTube trends and best practices. Attend webinars, read industry blogs, and continually learn to keep your channel growing and evolving.

Conclusion

Growing your YouTube channel to one million followers requires dedication, creativity, and strategic planning. By creating high-quality content, optimizing your channel, engaging with your audience, and leveraging various promotional strategies, you can build a successful YouTube presence. Stay consistent, monitor your progress, and be willing to adapt to the ever-changing landscape of YouTube.

Recommended Resources

- **YouTube Creator Academy**: Free educational resources to help you grow your YouTube channel.
- **TubeBuddy**: A browser extension that offers tools for optimizing and managing your YouTube content.
- **VidIQ**: A YouTube-certified tool that provides insights and analytics to help you improve your content strategy.
- **Canva**: A design tool for creating eye-catching thumbnails and channel art.
- **Hootsuite**: A social media management platform for scheduling posts and analyzing performance across different social networks.

By following the strategies outlined in this chapter, you can effectively grow your YouTube channel and achieve the milestone of one million followers.

Chapter 15: The best way to do Video Marketing in modern times

What is Video Marketing?

Video marketing is a strategic approach that uses video content to promote a brand, product, or service to a defined audience. It encompasses the creation, production, and distribution of videos to achieve marketing goals such as enhancing brand awareness, driving engagement, and increasing sales. This powerful medium leverages visual and auditory elements to communicate messages more effectively than traditional text-based content.

What are the Benefits of Video Marketing?

1. **Enhanced Engagement**: Videos capture attention and engage viewers more effectively than other content types. They can evoke emotions, tell stories, and simplify complex information, making them memorable and shareable.

2. **Boosted Conversion Rates**: Incorporating videos on landing pages or in emails can significantly increase conversion rates. Videos help build trust and credibility, encouraging viewers to take action.

3. **Improved SEO**: Videos can improve search engine rankings by increasing the time users spend on your site. Optimized videos with proper keywords can

also appear in video search results, driving more organic traffic.

4. **Increased Social Shares**: Videos are highly shareable on social media platforms. Engaging and entertaining videos can go viral, exponentially increasing your reach and brand visibility.

5. **Better Information Retention**: Viewers retain 95% of a message when they watch it in a video compared to just 10% when reading it in text. This makes videos an effective tool for educational and informational content.

6. **Humanized Brand**: Videos allow brands to showcase their personality, culture, and values, creating a stronger connection with the audience.

Who is Already Using Video Marketing?

Leading brands across various industries are leveraging video marketing to enhance their digital presence. Companies like Apple, Nike, and Coca-Cola regularly produce high-quality videos to promote their products, tell compelling stories, and engage with their audience. Small businesses and startups are also using video marketing to level the playing field, reaching potential customers without the need for large advertising budgets.

How Does Video Marketing Work?

1. **Strategy Development**: Define your goals, target audience, and key messages. Decide on the types of videos to create, such as tutorials, testimonials, product demos, or brand stories.

2. **Content Creation**: Plan, script, and produce your videos. Focus on creating high-quality, engaging content that aligns with your brand and resonates with your audience.

3. **Optimization**: Optimize your videos for search engines by including relevant keywords in titles, descriptions, and tags. Use compelling thumbnails and captions to attract more viewers.

4. **Distribution**: Share your videos across various platforms, including your website, social media, email campaigns, and video hosting sites like YouTube and Vimeo.

5. **Promotion**: Use paid advertising, influencer collaborations, and social media promotion to increase your video's reach and engagement.

6. **Analytics and Adjustment**: Monitor the performance of your videos using analytics tools. Track metrics like views, engagement, and conversion rates to understand what works and adjust your strategy accordingly.

Successful Videos for Marketing Strategies

1. **Product Demos and Tutorials**: Show how your product works and its benefits. These videos can help potential customers understand and appreciate your product, leading to increased sales.

2. **Customer Testimonials**: Feature satisfied customers sharing their positive experiences.

Testimonials build trust and credibility, influencing potential buyers.

3. **Behind-the-Scenes**: Give viewers a glimpse into your company culture, processes, or events. This humanizes your brand and builds a stronger connection with your audience.

4. **Explainer Videos**: Simplify complex concepts or processes with animated explainer videos. These are great for educational content and increasing understanding of your offerings.

5. **Live Videos**: Engage with your audience in real-time through live streaming. Host Q&A sessions, product launches, or live events to create immediate and interactive experiences.

Distributing Marketing Videos

1. **YouTube**: The largest video-sharing platform, ideal for reaching a broad audience. Optimize your channel and videos for better discoverability.

2. **Social Media**: Share videos on platforms like Facebook, Instagram, LinkedIn, and TikTok. Each platform has unique features and audiences, so tailor your content accordingly.

3. **Website and Blog**: Embed videos on your website and blog to enhance content and improve SEO. Use videos to complement text content and keep visitors engaged.

4. **Email Campaigns**: Incorporate videos into your email marketing to increase open rates and conversions. Personalized video messages can enhance customer relationships.

5. **Video Hosting Services**: Use platforms like Vimeo or Wistia for professional video hosting and advanced analytics. These services offer better control and customization options.

Conclusion

Video marketing is a versatile and impactful strategy that can significantly enhance your digital marketing efforts. By creating high-quality, engaging videos and effectively distributing them across various channels, you can reach a wider audience, build stronger connections, and drive better results for your business.

Next Steps

1. Develop a comprehensive video marketing strategy tailored to your goals and audience.

2. Invest in quality video production to ensure your content is professional and engaging.

3. Continuously analyze performance and adjust your strategy based on insights and feedback.

Recommended Resources

1. **HubSpot's Ultimate Guide to Video Marketing**: A comprehensive resource for mastering video marketing.

2. **Wistia's Learning Center**: Offers tutorials and tips on creating effective video content.

3. **Animoto's Blog**: Provides inspiration and ideas for video marketing strategies.

4. **Sprout Social**: Tools and resources for managing and analyzing your video marketing efforts.

Chapter 16: The best way to do LinkedIn Marketing in modern times

Introduction

LinkedIn has become an essential platform for professionals seeking to enhance their careers and businesses aiming to establish a strong online presence. This chapter will guide you through the ins and outs of LinkedIn marketing, ensuring you make the most out of this powerful tool without unnecessary hassle.

4 Benefits of Using LinkedIn

1. **Professional Networking**: LinkedIn connects you with professionals across various industries, allowing you to expand your network and open doors to new opportunities.

2. **Brand Visibility**: Regular updates and interactions on LinkedIn increase your brand's visibility, helping you establish authority in your field.

3. **Lead Generation**: LinkedIn's advanced search features and targeted advertising options make it an effective platform for generating high-quality leads.

4. **Recruitment**: Businesses can attract top talent by posting job openings and actively searching for qualified candidates.
5. **Industry Insights**: Follow industry leaders and join groups to stay updated on the latest trends and discussions in your field.

3 Misconceptions about LinkedIn

1. **LinkedIn is Only for Job Seekers**: While job hunting is a major use, LinkedIn also offers immense value for networking, brand building, and lead generation.
2. **LinkedIn Ads are Ineffective**: With precise targeting options, LinkedIn ads can be highly effective if used correctly.
3. **LinkedIn is Just an Online Resume**: Beyond your profile, LinkedIn provides tools for publishing content, engaging with your network, and joining professional groups.

Getting LinkedIn

1. **Creating a Compelling Profile**: Start with a professional photo and a headline that clearly states your value proposition. Write a summary that highlights your achievements, skills, and professional interests.
2. **Building Your Network**: Connect with colleagues, industry leaders, and potential clients. Personalize connection requests to increase acceptance rates.

3. **Engaging with Content**: Post regular updates, share industry news, and write articles to keep your network engaged. Comment on and share others' content to increase visibility.

5 Quick Tips for Success

1. **Consistency is Key**: Regular activity on LinkedIn helps keep you top of mind for your network.

2. **Use Keywords**: Optimize your profile with relevant keywords to improve searchability.

3. **Showcase Your Work**: Use the featured section to highlight presentations, projects, and articles.

4. **Join and Participate in Groups**: Engage in relevant groups to expand your network and establish authority.

5. **Leverage LinkedIn Analytics**: Use analytics to track the performance of your posts and adjust your strategy accordingly.

LinkedIn DIY Checklist

1. **Profile Optimization**: Ensure your profile is complete and up-to-date with a professional photo, headline, summary, and experience.

2. **Content Calendar**: Plan and schedule regular posts to maintain a consistent presence.

3. **Connection Strategy**: Identify and connect with key individuals in your industry.

4. **Engagement Plan**: Regularly engage with your network through comments, shares, and messages.

5. **Analytics Review**: Periodically review your LinkedIn analytics to assess the effectiveness of your efforts.

Questions to Ask a Social Media Consultant

1. **What is your experience with LinkedIn marketing?**
2. **Can you provide examples of successful LinkedIn campaigns you have managed?**
3. **How do you stay updated with LinkedIn's algorithm changes?**
4. **What tools do you use for LinkedIn analytics and automation?**
5. **How do you tailor LinkedIn strategies for different industries?**
6. **What are your recommendations for increasing engagement on LinkedIn?**
7. **How do you handle negative feedback or comments on LinkedIn?**

LinkedIn is a robust platform for professionals and businesses alike, offering numerous opportunities for growth and engagement. By understanding its benefits, dispelling common misconceptions, and following practical tips, you can harness the full potential of LinkedIn marketing without tears. Keep your profile updated, engage consistently, and leverage analytics to refine your strategy, ensuring sustained success on LinkedIn.

Chapter 17: Marketing Consultant

Introduction

Navigating the intricate landscape of marketing can be challenging for businesses of all sizes. This is where the expertise of a marketing consultant becomes invaluable. A marketing consultant provides specialized knowledge and strategies tailored to meet the unique needs of a business, enhancing its marketing efforts and driving growth.

What is a Marketing Consultant?

A marketing consultant is a professional who analyzes a company's current marketing strategies and develops and implements new plans to improve engagement and sales. They bring a wealth of knowledge and experience from various industries, enabling them to offer fresh perspectives and innovative solutions. Their role can encompass everything from market research and strategy development to campaign execution and performance analysis.

Why Hire a Marketing Consultant?

4 benefits of hiring a marketing consultant:

1. **Expertise and Experience:** They provide specialized skills and industry knowledge that might be lacking in-house.

2. **Objective Perspective:** Consultants can offer unbiased insights and identify issues that internal teams might overlook.

3. **Cost-Effective:** Hiring a consultant can be more economical than employing a full-time marketing specialist.

4. **Flexibility:** Consultants can be hired on a project basis, providing flexibility to scale efforts up or down as needed.

5 Different Types of Marketing

Marketing is a broad field with various specialties. Understanding these can help businesses identify the type of consultant they need:

1. **Digital Marketing:** Focuses on online channels such as social media, email, SEO, and content marketing.

2. **Brand Marketing:** Involves building and maintaining a brand's image and reputation.

3. **Content Marketing:** Centers on creating and distributing valuable content to attract and engage a target audience.

4. **Product Marketing:** Deals with promoting and selling a product to a specific market.

5. **Event Marketing:** Involves organizing events to promote a product, service, or brand.

4 Things You Should Consider Before Hiring a Marketing Consultant

Before hiring a marketing consultant, consider the following:

1. **Business Needs:** Clearly define your marketing goals and what you hope to achieve with a consultant.

2. **Budget:** Determine how much you are willing to invest in a consultant.

3. **Experience and Expertise:** Look for consultants with experience in your industry and a proven track record of success.

4. **Compatibility:** Ensure their working style and values align with your company culture.

How Do You Find a Marketing Consultant?

Finding the right marketing consultant involves:

1. **Research:** Look for consultants with good reviews and case studies.

2. **Referrals:** Ask for recommendations from your professional network.

3. **Directories and Agencies:** Use directories and marketing agencies to find reputable consultants.

4. **Interviews:** Conduct interviews to assess their suitability for your needs.

Questions to Ask a Marketing Consultant

When interviewing potential consultants, ask questions such as:

1. **What is your experience in our industry?**
2. **Can you provide case studies or references?**
3. **What strategies do you suggest for our business?**
4. **How do you measure success?**
5. **What is your fee structure?**

The Costs of a Marketing Consultant

The cost of hiring a marketing consultant can vary based on their experience, expertise, and the scope of work. Typical pricing models include:

1. **Hourly Rate:** Ideal for short-term projects or consultations.
2. **Project-Based:** A flat fee for a specific project.
3. **Retainer:** A monthly fee for ongoing services.

What to Look for When Signing the Final Contract

Before signing a contract, ensure it includes:

1. **Scope of Work:** Clearly defined deliverables and timelines.
2. **Payment Terms:** Detailed fee structure and payment schedule.

3. **Confidentiality Agreement:** Protection of your business's sensitive information.
4. **Termination Clause:** Terms under which the contract can be terminated.

Questions to Ask Any Marketing Consultant

Here are additional questions to consider:

1. **How will you integrate with our existing team?**
2. **What tools and technologies do you use?**
3. **How do you stay updated with marketing trends?**
4. **What is your approach to dealing with challenges?**

Conclusion

Hiring a marketing consultant can provide the expertise and strategic direction needed to elevate your marketing efforts. By understanding their role, the different types of marketing, and what to consider when hiring, businesses can make informed decisions that lead to successful partnerships and improved marketing outcomes.

Recommended Resources

1. **MarketingProfs:** Offers a wealth of resources on marketing strategies and best practices.
2. **HubSpot Academy:** Provides free online courses on various aspects of marketing.

3. **American Marketing Association (AMA):** A professional association offering networking opportunities and industry insights.

Chapter 18: Managing Your Online Reputation

Why is Your Online Reputation Important?

In today's digital age, your online reputation is critical. It shapes how potential customers, partners, and stakeholders perceive your brand. A positive online reputation can enhance credibility, attract more customers, and build trust. Conversely, a negative reputation can harm your business, leading to loss of customers and revenue.

Assessing Your Online Reputation

Before you can manage your online reputation, you need to assess it. Start by conducting a thorough audit of your online presence. Search for your business on search engines, review sites, and social media platforms. Pay attention to reviews, comments, and mentions. Tools like Google Alerts, Social Mention, and Brandwatch can help you monitor your online reputation in real-time.

How to Hire an Internet Marketing Consultant

Hiring an internet marketing consultant can be a game-changer for managing your online reputation. Here's a step-by-step guide:

1. **Identify Your Needs**: Clearly define what you want to achieve. Do you need help with SEO, social media, content marketing, or all of the above?

2. **Research Potential Consultants**: Look for consultants with a strong track record. Check their portfolios, case studies, and client testimonials.

3. **Evaluate Expertise**: Ensure the consultant has experience in your industry and understands your business needs.

4. **Check References**: Ask for references and contact them to verify the consultant's credibility and performance.

Questions to Ask an Internet Marketing Consultant

When interviewing potential consultants, ask the following questions:

1. Can you provide examples of past success stories?
2. What strategies do you use to manage online reputations?
3. How do you measure the success of your campaigns?
4. Can you provide a detailed plan for improving our online reputation?
5. What tools and technologies do you use?

How to Build Your Online Reputation

Building a strong online reputation requires a proactive approach:

1. **Create High-Quality Content**: Regularly publish informative and engaging content that adds value to your audience.

2. **Engage with Your Audience**: Respond to comments, reviews, and messages promptly. Show appreciation for positive feedback and address negative feedback constructively.

3. **Leverage Social Media**: Use social media platforms to connect with your audience, share content, and showcase your brand's personality.

4. **Encourage Reviews**: Ask satisfied customers to leave positive reviews on platforms like Google, Yelp, and Trustpilot.

5. **Monitor Your Reputation**: Continuously monitor your online presence to quickly address any issues that arise.

How to Protect Your Online Reputation

Protecting your online reputation involves:

1. **Regular Monitoring**: Use tools like Google Alerts and Mention to stay updated on what's being said about your brand.

2. **Responding to Feedback**: Address negative comments and reviews promptly and professionally.

3. **Creating Positive Content**: Counteract negative content by publishing positive news, customer testimonials, and success stories.

4. **Building Relationships**: Foster strong relationships with customers, influencers, and industry leaders who can vouch for your brand.

ORM Best Business Practices

1. **Transparency**: Be honest and transparent in all your communications.

2. **Consistency**: Maintain a consistent brand voice across all platforms.

3. **Proactivity**: Address potential issues before they escalate.

4. **Customer-Centric Approach**: Focus on providing exceptional customer service.

Questions to Ask an Internet Marketing Consultant Checklist

1. What is your experience in our industry?

2. Can you provide references from past clients?

3. What specific services do you offer for online reputation management?

4. How do you stay updated with the latest trends and changes in digital marketing?

5. What is your process for handling negative reviews and feedback?

ORM Best Business Practices Checklist

1. Monitor your online presence regularly.
2. Engage with your audience consistently.
3. Publish high-quality, positive content.
4. Address negative feedback promptly.
5. Build strong relationships with key stakeholders.

Next Steps

1. Implement the strategies outlined in this chapter.
2. Continuously monitor and adjust your approach based on feedback and results.
3. Stay updated with the latest trends in online reputation management.

Recommended Resources

1. **Google Alerts**: Set up alerts to monitor your online mentions.
2. **Hootsuite**: Manage your social media presence and engage with your audience.
3. **Canva**: Create professional graphics for your content.

4. **Trustpilot**: Manage and respond to customer reviews.

5. **Brandwatch**: Track your online reputation and gain insights into public sentiment.

Conclusion

Recap of Key Points

Throughout this book, we have explored the multifaceted world of digital marketing, delving into its various components, strategies, and tools. We began with an understanding of digital marketing, covering the basics and its importance in today's business landscape. We then moved on to specific tactics such as search engine optimization (SEO), content marketing, social media marketing, email marketing, pay-per-click (PPC) advertising, and the role of artificial intelligence (AI) in enhancing these strategies.

We discussed the critical aspects of building a strong online presence, from creating a user-friendly website to optimizing for mobile and crafting a compelling brand identity. We highlighted the significance of high-quality content and the development of a comprehensive content strategy, exploring different content types and distribution channels.

In the realm of social media, we examined the process of selecting the right platforms, creating engaging content, leveraging social media advertising, and utilizing tools for effective management. Our exploration of email marketing included building and segmenting email lists, crafting effective campaigns, and analyzing key metrics for continuous improvement.

Our focus on PPC advertising provided insights into creating and managing campaigns, analyzing performance, and using essential tools for optimization. Finally, we covered analytics and data-driven marketing, emphasizing the importance of data, tools for data collection and analysis, making data-driven decisions, and tracking key metrics.

Future of Digital Marketing

The future of digital marketing is poised for continued evolution, driven by technological advancements and changing consumer behaviors. Here are some key trends and innovations that will shape the future of digital marketing:

1. **Increased Use of Artificial Intelligence:**
    - AI will continue to play a pivotal role in personalizing marketing efforts, automating tasks, and providing deeper insights through data analysis. Advanced AI algorithms will enable more precise targeting and improved customer experiences [2].

2. **Voice Search Optimization:**
    - With the growing popularity of smart speakers and voice assistants, optimizing for voice search will become essential. Marketers will need to focus on natural language processing and conversational queries to stay relevant [5].

3. **Rise of Augmented Reality (AR) and Virtual Reality (VR):**
    - AR and VR will offer immersive experiences, allowing brands to engage customers in new and innovative ways. These technologies will be particularly impactful in sectors like retail, real estate, and entertainment [6].

4. **Continued Growth of Video Marketing:**
   - Video content will remain a dominant force, with live streaming, short-form videos, and interactive content gaining traction. Platforms like YouTube, TikTok, and Instagram will continue to evolve, providing more opportunities for video marketing [4].

5. **Enhanced Data Privacy and Security:**
   - With increasing concerns over data privacy, marketers will need to prioritize transparency and compliance with regulations like GDPR and CCPA. Building trust with consumers through ethical data practices will be crucial [1].

6. **Integration of Blockchain Technology:**
   - Blockchain can enhance transparency and security in digital marketing, particularly in areas like ad verification, supply chain transparency, and data protection. Its adoption will drive more secure and trustworthy marketing practices [3].

Final Thoughts and Next Steps

As we conclude this book, it's essential to recognize that digital marketing is a dynamic and ever-evolving field.

Staying ahead requires continuous learning, adaptation, and a willingness to embrace new technologies and strategies.

5 steps to help you succeed in your digital marketing journey:

1. **Stay Informed:**
    - Keep up with the latest trends, tools, and best practices in digital marketing. Follow industry blogs, attend webinars, and participate in professional networks to stay updated.

2. **Experiment and Innovate:**
    - Don't be afraid to try new approaches and experiment with different tactics. Innovation often leads to breakthrough results, so be open to testing and iterating on your strategies.

3. **Invest in Skills Development:**
    - Continuously enhance your skills and knowledge through online courses, certifications, and workshops. Building expertise in areas like SEO, content creation, social media management, and data analytics will give you a competitive edge.

4. **Leverage Analytics:**

- Use data and analytics to measure the effectiveness of your campaigns and make informed decisions. Regularly review your performance metrics and adjust your strategies based on insights.

5. **Focus on the Customer:**
    - Always keep the customer at the center of your digital marketing efforts. Understand their needs, preferences, and behaviors, and tailor your strategies to provide value and enhance their experience.

By following these steps and embracing a mindset of continuous improvement, you can navigate the complexities of digital marketing and achieve long-term success.

Appendix

Glossary of Digital Marketing Terms

A/B Testing: A method of comparing two versions of a webpage or app against each other to determine which one performs better.

AdWords: Google's advertising system in which advertisers bid on certain keywords for their clickable ads to appear in Google's search results.

Analytics: The systematic computational analysis of data or statistics. In digital marketing, it often refers to website analytics, tracking metrics such as page views, time on site, and conversion rates.

Backlink: An incoming hyperlink from one web page to another website. Backlinks are important for SEO because search engines see multiple backlinks as a sign that the content is worth linking to, and thus also worth ranking well on a search engine result page (SERP).

Bounce Rate: The percentage of visitors to a particular website who navigate away from the site after viewing only one page.

Call to Action (CTA): A prompt on a website that tells the user to take some specified action. Example: "Buy Now" or "Sign Up."

Click-Through Rate (CTR): The ratio of users who click on a specific link to the number of total users who view a page, email, or advertisement.

Content Management System (CMS): A software application or set of related programs that are used to create and manage digital content. Examples include WordPress, Joomla, and Drupal.

Conversion Rate: The percentage of users who take a desired action. This could be filling out a form, making a purchase, or signing up for a newsletter.

Cost Per Click (CPC): A method that websites use to bill advertisers based on the number of times a visitor clicks on an advertisement.

Digital Marketing: The use of the internet, mobile devices, social media, search engines, and other channels to reach consumers.

Email Marketing: The act of sending a commercial message, typically to a group of people, using email.

Engagement Rate: A metric that measures the level of engagement that a piece of created content is receiving from an audience.

Influencer Marketing: A type of social media marketing that uses endorsements and product mentions from influencers–individuals who have a dedicated social following and are viewed as experts within their niche.

Keyword: A significant word or phrase, relevant to the content on a website, that is used in search engine optimization to attract traffic to the website.

Landing Page: A standalone web page created specifically for a marketing or advertising campaign. It's where a visitor "lands" after they click on a link in an email or ads from

Google, Bing, YouTube, Facebook, Instagram, Twitter, or similar places on the web.

Pay-Per-Click (PPC): An internet advertising model used to drive traffic to websites, in which an advertiser pays a publisher when the ad is clicked.

Search Engine Optimization (SEO): The process of optimizing a website to rank higher in search engine results pages (SERPs), which increases the visibility of the site.

Social Media Marketing: The use of social media platforms and websites to promote a product or service.

User Experience (UX): The overall experience of a person using a product such as a website or computer application, especially in terms of how easy or pleasing it is to use.

List of Useful Digital Marketing Tools

Google Analytics: A web analytics service offered by Google that tracks and reports website traffic, currently as a platform inside the Google Marketing Platform brand.

SEMrush: A software as a service (SaaS) platform used for keyword research and online ranking data, including metrics such as search volume and cost per click (CPC).

Ahrefs: A toolset for SEO and marketing running on big data. It is mainly used for checking backlinks, tracking keywords, and auditing websites.

Mailchimp: An American marketing automation platform and email marketing service for managing mailing lists and creating email marketing campaigns.

Hootsuite: A social media management platform that allows users to schedule and post updates to any pages or profiles they have on social networks.

Buffer: A software application for the web and mobile, designed to manage accounts in social networks, by providing the means for a user to schedule posts to Twitter, Facebook, Instagram, and LinkedIn.

Moz: A software as a service (SaaS) company based in Seattle, Washington, USA, that sells inbound marketing and marketing analytics software subscriptions.

Canva: A graphic design platform, used to create social media graphics, presentations, posters, documents, and other visual content.

HubSpot: A developer and marketer of software products for inbound marketing, sales, and customer service.

BuzzSumo: A tool that allows you to find the most shared content and key influencers to promote your content.

Additional Resources for Further Learning

Coursera - Digital Marketing Specialization:

- A comprehensive online course covering various aspects of digital marketing, including SEO, social media marketing, and analytics. Coursera Digital Marketing

Google Digital Garage:

- Free courses on everything from search to social media, to help you grow your business or career. Google Digital Garage

HubSpot Academy:

- Free online training for inbound marketing, sales, and customer service professionals. HubSpot Academy

Moz SEO Learning Center:

- An extensive resource for learning about SEO and how to implement effective SEO strategies. Moz SEO Learning Center

Content Marketing Institute:

- Provides a wealth of resources and training on content marketing. Content Marketing Institute

www.ingramcontent.com/pod-product-compliance
Lightning Source LLC
Chambersburg PA
CBHW070437180526
45158CB00019B/1494